Spies and Spying

HOW SPIES WORK

K.C. Kelley

A+
Smart Apple Media

Smart Apple Media
P.O. Box 3263, Mankato, MN 56002

Printed in the United States of America

Library of Congress Cataloging-in-Publication Data

Kelley, K. C.
  How spies work / K.C. Kelley.
     p. cm. -- (Spies and spying)
  Includes index.
  ISBN 978-1-59920-359-1 (hardcover)
  1. Espionage--Juvenile literature. 2. Spies--Juvenile literature. I. Title.
  UB270.5.K45 2010
  327.12--dc22

                                              2008049279

Created by Q2AMedia
Editor: Honor Head
Art Director: Rahul Dhiman
Designer: Ranjan Singh
Picture Researcher: Shreya Sharma
Line Artist: Sibi N. Devasia
Coloring Artist: Mahender Kumar

All words in **bold** can be found in the glossary on pages 30–31.

Web site information is correct at time of going to press. However, the publishers cannot
accept liability for any information or links found on third-party web sites.

Picture credits
t=top b=bottom c=center l=left r=right

Cover: Michael Crockett Photography/ Photolibrary, Marjan Laznik/ iStockphoto, Q2A Media Art Bank.

Insides: Marjan Laznik/ iStockphoto: Title Page, Andrew Howe/ iStockphoto: 4l, Peter Hince/ Stone/Getty Images: 5t,
Michael Ledray/ Shutterstock: 5b, Jamie McDonald/ Getty Images: 6r, Marjan Laznik/ iStockphoto: 7b, Gramper/ Bigstockphoto:
8r, Olivier Le Queinec/ Dreamstime: 8b, Mark Stout/ Dreamstime: 9r, Michael Crockett Photography/ Photolibrary: 10b, Ursula/
Shutterstock: 11t, SSG Bronco Suzuki/ Defence Imagery.Mil: 11b, Mark Finkenstaedt: 12r, Shutterstock: 13b, Ed Holub/ Photolibrary:
14b, Lars Topelmann/ Photolibrary: 15b, Rob Lang/ Photolibrary: 16l, Dennis Cook/ Associated Press: 17l, FBI/ U.S. Federal
Government/ U.S. Department of Justice.: 17b, Clarence S Lewis/ Shutterstock: 18b, National Security Agency/ Central Security
Service: 19t, Evening Standard/ Hulton Archive/ Getty Images: 19b, National Archives: 20t, National Archives: 21l, Dhoxax/
Shutterstock: 23t, Norman Chan/ Shutterstock: 23b, STR/ Associated Press: 24r, Dave Bartruff/ Corbis: 25t, Owen Price/ iStockphoto:
27b, Krzysztof Zmij/ iStockphoto: 28r, C. Benton: 28b, NASA Images: 29b, Andrew Howe/ iStockphoto: 31.

Q2A Media Art Bank: 7, 9, 13, 17, 20, 22, 25, 26.

9 8 7 6 5 4 3 2 1

CONTENTS

Spies at Work.............................. 4

Spy Skills 6

In the Shadows 8

Stealing Secrets 10

Those Who Know...................... 14

Sending Secrets Home................ 18

Tricks of the Trade.................... 22

Fighting Back 26

High-Tech Spying 28

Glossary 30

Index and Web Finder................ 32

SPIES AT WORK

For centuries, rulers and governments have had secrets that other people want to know about. This is why nearly every country has spies—to find out things people don't want found out!

Working in Secret

Governments have many secrets, such as plans for war, deadly weapons, or other important information. Enemies of those governments want to uncover those secrets. To do this, they turn to the silent experts— spies. A spy usually works for one side against another, finding hidden information. Being a spy can be exciting, but it can also be dangerous.

Spies use everyday equipment such as binoculars to find secrets.

Spies must learn to follow people without being noticed to find out information.

Nathan Hale

One of America's first spies was Nathan Hale. He was sent to spy on the British in New York during the **Revolutionary War.** Hale was captured and hanged by the British in 1776. Before he died he said: "I regret that I have only one life to give for my country."

The Quiet Service

Spies have many skills. They have to learn where secret information is kept and how to access that information. Spies have to be a combination of burglars, con artists, technical wizards, language experts, and even great shots.

Top Secret

FOR YOUR EYES ONLY

Some secrets are more secret than others. Secrets are separated into:
- "Secret" files—may be shared by others in the organization
- Top Secret—only to be seen by a very limited group
- For Your Eyes Only—not to be shown to anyone else at all

SPY SKILLS

How do you become a spy? Like any tough job, there's a lot to learn! Training is hard, and you need to build up lots of skills, from acting to shooting!

Getting Fit

Spies have to be physically fit. Organizations that train spies, such as the **CIA**, have tough training programs. Trainee spies practice using weapons and learn face-to-face fighting. Spies often have to pretend to be someone else, so they must learn how to make different facial expressions and body movements. Learning how to act is an important part of their training.

Spies must be able to escape from tricky situations. They train hard to learn how to climb ropes, swim rivers, or even dig tunnels.

Getting Brainy

Spies spend more time in classrooms than they do in the gym. They learn languages they might need to speak if they are going to a foreign country and tricks such as how to disguise themselves. They practice making and breaking codes and they work with experts in radio and other technology that will help them **intercept** secrets. If they are going to be sent to a new country, they carefully study maps and other information about their destination.

SPY FILE

Stella Rimington

Many women have been top spies or have worked in the secret services. In 1992, Stella Rimington was the first woman to lead a national spy agency. She ran Britain's **MI5** organization. She now writes best-selling detective thrillers.

Top Secret

Both sides in any war know that the other side is using spies. If one side captures an enemy spy, the government sometimes uses the spy to bargain. They might agree to swap the captured spy in exchange for information or for one of their own captured spies.

Learning to use firearms is an important skill for many spies. But guns are used only when absolutely necessary.

Nappanee Elem. Media Center
Nappanee, IN

IN THE SHADOWS

Once training is done, a spy has to go out into the field to uncover the secret information that is needed. But those secrets are usually well hidden.

Finding Secrets

The first step for a spy is to find out where the secrets or information are hidden. To do this, the spy may try to win the trust and friendship of his enemies so that they reveal information by mistake. But this could take a long time. It might be quicker for a spy to search the building where the secrets are held. For instance, there is a good chance that the plans for a new rocket could be in a government science building.

Where are secrets kept? Often behind locked doors. Spies carry special tools like these "lock picks" to break open doors and locks.

Top Secret

Picking a lock means opening it without using the key. With most locks, it is easy for a trained spy. New electronic locks, however, are harder to open. Now spies have to use special electronic cards that can read the locks' combinations.

Breaking In

When they know where the secrets are kept, spies have to wait for dark, or for a time when the building is empty, to search it. To reach their target building, spies might have to talk with a guard, put on a disguise, or pretend to be someone who works there. They might have to pick a lock, scale a wall, or break a window. They do whatever it takes to get inside safely and quietly.

Breaking into buildings quickly and quietly is a special spy skill.

SPY FILE

Jonathan Pollard

In 1985, an employee of the U.S. Navy named Jonathan Pollard was caught with a briefcase that held 60 **classified** documents. Many were stamped "Top Secret." It was discovered that Pollard had been smuggling out military secrets and selling them to Israeli agents and others for more than a year.

STEALING SECRETS

What happens when the spy has found a pile of secret papers? This is where tiny spy cameras come in really handy.

Eye Spy

In many cases, spies have to steal information without anyone knowing it's been stolen. So instead of sneaking out with a case of documents, they have to photograph the papers. Spy cameras are very small. They work in areas without much light and are small enough to carry without being noticed.

Taking a picture of a secret document instead of stealing the document can keep the other side from knowing that the spy has been there!

Caught on Camera

Sometimes spies want to record something they know will happen when they're not around. For this, they can use tiny video cameras. Miniature video cameras have a lens that is no bigger than a pencil end. They are small enough to be hidden in desk lamps, potted plants, clocks, or paintings. The spy hides the video camera so it can't be seen but can still record. The spy can then watch what happens from a safe distance. Later, the video can also be used as evidence or **blackmail**!

A camera small enough to be tucked in a pocket can take top-quality pictures and videos silently and quickly.

f=4.45mm F2.8

Top Secret

Photographs need light. But what do you do if you can't use a light because that would give you away? You use a special night vision camera that takes pictures in near darkness.

You could also use night vision glasses that let you "see" in the dark —very useful when sneaking around buildings in the dead of night.

Hidden Bugs

If you can't take a picture of a secret, you might be able to hear it. Spies used to hide inside rooms and hope to overhear something. But now spies can hide **microphones** or **bugs** in just about anything. Bugs are used to record conversations and are tiny enough to be hidden in an electrical socket, a calculator, or under a phone. The Soviet Union once sent a carving to hang on the wall of the U.S. Embassy in Moscow. Inside the carving was a hidden microphone!

Top Secret

If you can't plant a bug in an office, you might still be able to listen in. Special devices shoot laser beams at windows. The windows vibrate when there is noise or talking inside the room. The laser "reads" the vibrations and translates them into sound which you can hear. Clever!

Powerful microphones can be concealed just about anywhere. This mic was placed inside a fake tree stump to record a conversation outdoors.

Phone Taps

People do a lot of talking on the telephone, so "tapping" into those conversations can reveal many secrets. Spies plant bugs in phones, phone lines, and phone poles. These bugs either tape the conversation or send them to another phone where the spy can listen in. Calls from cell phones can be intercepted, too. Also, as more and more people use computers to make calls, spies are starting to listen in using special software bugs.

SPY FILE

Bugged!

In the late 1940s, the FBI wanted to prove that Judy Conlon was a Soviet spy. To do this, FBI agents planted bugs in her home and office. By listening to her plot with other agents, they gathered enough evidence to arrest and convict her.

Sounds recorded by hidden microphones can be read as sound waves like the ones shown here. These sound waves can also be analyzed by electronic machines to make them clearer.

THOSE WHO KNOW

Sometimes the information needed is more difficult to find. To get these secrets, spies have to be more creative. Some have to go undercover.

Secrets for Money

One of the best ways to get secret information is simply to buy it. People who know secrets will sometimes pass that information to a spy for cash. The person who provides the secrets won't give the spy away, either. If they did, they would be in serious trouble with the people they had stolen the secrets from.

Some people have made a lot of money by selling secrets for cash.

Blackmail!

Not all people will be tempted by money. Sometimes they have to be forced to tell their secrets. Threatening to reveal a personal secret about someone—such as a crime in their past—is called blackmail. It can be used to make someone give you what you want— but first you have to find something to blackmail them with.

Spies will use threats or blackmail to force people to give them secret information.

SPY FILE

Undercover

In the early 1980s, a team of Israeli spies set up a business in Khartoum, Sudan, pretending to be travel resort owners. But they were really bribing government officials to let them smuggle Jewish people out of Ethiopia. The Jewish people were being oppressed by their government, so the Israeli spies used money and a clever plan to save them.

Beware, Moles

Another way to find out secrets is to recruit a **mole**. Moles pretend to work for one side when they are actually working for the enemy side. Unlike other spies, moles get jobs working for the enemy's intelligence agencies. They can do a lot of damage by passing on secrets and information to their own people. A mole can be in place for years without being discovered.

A mole is a spy who spends many years pretending to work for the enemy.

Top Secret

One of the most successful spy operations ever used moles. Operation Double Cross was run by the British government during World War II. Early in the war, British intelligence discovered German agents working in Britain. Instead of putting them in jail, they put them to work. The British used these double agents to send false information to Germany for years.

Master Mole

Moles often place their own lives at risk. In 1960, Oleg Penkovsky, a top Soviet intelligence official, became a mole for Western intelligence agencies. He passed dozens of pieces of information to the CIA and **MI6** about Soviet plans for nuclear weapons. He became one of the United States' most valuable spies. The **KGB** eventually caught him and put him on trial. He was found guilty and executed in 1963.

Oleg Penkovsky wanted to prevent nuclear war by sharing Soviet military secrets.

SPY FILE

Kim Philby

Perhaps the most famous mole of all time was Kim Philby. For more than 20 years, he secretly passed information to the Soviet intelligence service while working for the British government. By the 1950s, he was under suspicion. Finally, in 1963, Philby escaped to the Soviet Union, where he lived until his death in 1988.

17

SENDING SECRETS HOME

Once they've got the secrets, spies have to get them to their bosses safely. Spies have to be just as careful sending information as finding it.

Using Codes

One way to send information that no one else can read is to put it in code. But it has to be done in a way that the person receiving it can decode the message. Learning how to code and decode messages is a big part of a spy's work. Codes might be simply switching letters around, or the use of symbols instead of letters. Other codes might use a "key" that has been carefully thought out by the intelligence agency.

以内时：
爱尔兰、列支敦士登、墨西哥、瑞士、英国(不包括英国殖民地发出的护照)

月以内时：
智利、哥斯达黎加、克罗地亚、塞浦路斯、丹麦、多米尼加、萨尔瓦
以色列、意大利、莱索托、卢森堡、马其顿、马耳他、毛里求斯
地发出的护照)、圣马利诺、新加坡、斯洛文尼亚、西班牙、

以内时
利亚、田
国、香

亚、匈牙利、拉脱维亚、立陶宛、摩纳哥、新西兰

申请取得签证。持有这类签证的人可以在日之
逗留者签证"。持有这类签证的人可以在日之
和领取报酬的活动，则日本政府不会发出这些

时候不管其访日目的必须提交下列文件：

Codes can be written in any language. This Chinese text could have characters switched around to give a spy a secret message.

Top Secret

Early in World War II, British military leaders knew that if they could crack the German code, they could gain a huge advantage. Using a captured German Enigma code machine, a team of some of the greatest minds in England gathered at a mansion in Bletchley Park, outside London. For nearly the entire war, they worked in complete secrecy. They decoded German information and saved thousands of lives.

Breaking a Code

Intelligence agencies use experts in **cryptography** to study and break enemy codes. Today, code breakers have computers to help them to decode enemy messages.

In this building and others at Bletchley Park in England, code breakers helped the **Allies** win World War II.

Using Radios

During World War II, the U.S. Army used native Navajo speakers to pass messages that the enemy could not translate.

Ever since radio was invented, spies have been using it to stay in touch with their bosses. Often they would transmit at an agreed time. The spy might just say his or her message or use **Morse code** to tap out the message, which would then be decoded at the other end.

Top Secret

Robert Baden Powell (1857–1941), pretended to study butterflies on spying trips abroad. He'd sketch a butterfly, which was really a plan of an enemy building. This butterfly shows the plan of an enemy **fortress.** The patch in the middle is the layout while the markings show the size and position of the guns.

Hidden Radios

Before cell phones, a spy's radio was his most important tool. Radios could be hidden in many ways, such as behind cabinets, under floors, or inside small briefcases. The **antennas** for these radios might have been disguised as TV antennas, stereo speaker wires, or even clotheslines. Spies were taught how to work the radios and how to fix them if they broke.

Morse Code

In the 1830s, Samuel F. B. Morse created a way for people to send messages by telegraph. The telegraph sent electrical signals along a wire. Morse thought of a way to make those signals into words. In his code, a person taps in dots or dashes that represent different letters of the alphabet. A machine at the other end taps out the same code, which is then "read" by someone listening. Morse code is still used today.

Radios and transmitters can be hidden in many places. An enemy searching a spy might not think to look in the heel of his shoe for this transmitter.

TRICKS OF THE TRADE

If you are constantly being watched and followed, passing on secrets can be a problem. However, there are a few tricks every spy knows.

Dead Drops

The most common way to pass messages between spies and their **controllers** is the **dead drop**. For instance, a dead drop might be under a park bench. The spy will let the controller know when and where the package will be. The spy then leaves it there. Later, the controller will collect the package. This way the spy and the controller never meet.

A chalk mark on a tree shows where a dead drop might be placed.

Passing in Public

Sometimes there's no time to arrange a dead drop, so spies have to "pass" secrets. This means that the spy and the controller meet in public but do not to speak or even seem to know each other. They pass very close to one another, on a busy street, for example. The spy slips the message to the controller without anyone seeing. This might be done by putting the message into a pocket or shopping bag.

Expert passing is done so well that anyone watching will not see that something has been passed.

Top Secret

One way that spies used to pass messages was through the newspaper. They would place a small ad in the paper, using everyday language but containing a code word. A fellow spy would read the ad, see the code word, and know that something was waiting for him at the dead drop.

Disguises

Another way that a spy might stay out of sight is by staying in disguise. Some spies use fake beards and mustaches, color their hair, and wear colored contact lenses and other disguise aids to make them look completely different. They might use a cane or even wear a fake cast to pretend they have a broken leg or arm. One male spy in France in the 1750s pretended to be a woman for more than 30 years in order to spy on the British!

These photos show the many different looks of German spy Dieter Kunzelmann.

Top Secret

In 1980, Antonio Mendez, head of disguise at the CIA, helped six people disguise themselves so that they could leave an embassy in Iran where they were being held **hostage**.

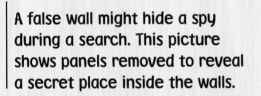

A false wall might hide a spy during a search. This picture shows panels removed to reveal a secret place inside the walls.

Hiding Places

Sometimes a spy has to hide out. Many spies living in an enemy country build false rooms into their homes or have a small chamber hidden under the floorboards. Other spies have used trunks or barrels to mail themselves home after their spy missions were over. Mary Queen of Scots (1542–1587) used spies in barrels to help plan her escapes. German agents during World War II parachuted into England inside barrel-shaped containers.

SPY FILE

Antonio Mendez

Antonio Mendez was a master at making people look like someone else. For more than 30 years, he made sure that CIA agents could hide almost anywhere. Today, Mendez gives lectures and writes books on his adventures.

FIGHTING BACK

Being caught is almost worse than being killed. A spy caught by the enemy might be forced to work for them and betray his own country.

Secret Weapons

Spies hope never to have to use weapons, but have to be ready to defend themselves if trapped by the enemy. Weapons have to be carefully disguised. Guns can be hidden inside lipstick tubes, walking sticks, belts, pens, or inside shoes in hollow heels. A wire attached to a wristwatch can be used to choke a guard.

Top Secret

One way that a spy can fight back is with a simple piece of jewelry—the killer ring. This ring is pretty from one side only. The inside edge is as sharp as a knife and can be used to slash an attacker.

This tiny gun could be hidden inside a glove.

Ka-boom!

Sometimes the worst way to hurt your enemy is not to steal their secrets . . . but just to blow the secrets up! Spies who destroy information are called **saboteurs**. They might sneak in to a military post at night and plant a time bomb that will go off hours later. Learning how to make and conceal explosives is part of a spy's training. They can take household chemicals and an alarm clock and make a lot of trouble behind enemy lines.

SPY FILE

Saboteurs in WWII

During World War II, a plant in Norway had an ingredient the Nazis needed to make nuclear weapons. Norwegian saboteurs got plans of the building and snuck in through a basement window. They placed bombs in the building and escaped before the explosion.

Spies usually do not try to blow up people, just places. They might use special materials, such as wire and plastic explosive, to make a time bomb.

HIGH-TECH SPYING

Today's spies have a huge range of electronic and technical equipment they can use to make spying more efficient and safer.

Hacker Spies

The use of computers has made spying a bit safer. Spies can "hack" into the computer networks of their enemies to find secrets. They use software that helps them disable passwords. They might also write a program that disguises their true identity and allows them to pretend to be a part of the enemy's network. Today computer security against government or industrial spies is big business.

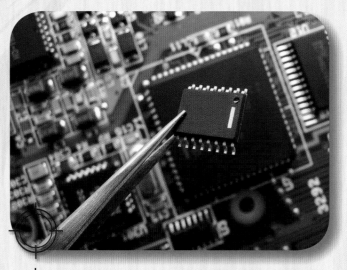

Huge amounts of information can be stored on tiny computer chips. Instead of snapping pictures of secret papers, today's spies steal these chips.

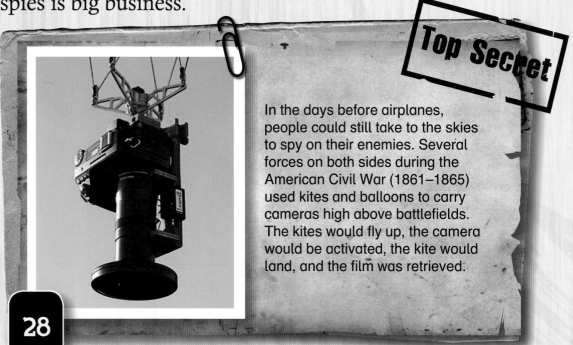

Top Secret

In the days before airplanes, people could still take to the skies to spy on their enemies. Several forces on both sides during the American Civil War (1861–1865) used kites and balloons to carry cameras high above battlefields. The kites would fly up, the camera would be activated, the kite would land, and the film was retrieved.

Satellite Spying

Another way of safe spying is through the use of satellites. In space, they orbit the Earth and aim super-cameras at military bases in enemy countries. The satellites might track shipments of valuable cargo at sea or follow the enemy's troop movements.

Photos like this one of land in Egypt are taken by satellites. Spies can examine the photos to learn more about life in their enemy's country.

SPY FILE

Anti-terrorism

Many spies today fight terrorism and illegal activities. In 1992, police used spies to capture Abimael Guzman. His group, called Shining Path, killed more than 25,000 people in Peru over 20 years. Police planted a mole in his group who collected intelligence and worked in disguise as part of their plan to bring him to justice.

land

sea

forest

GLOSSARY

Allies countries including the United States, France, Australia, Great Britain, and Russia that fought on the same side during World War II

antennas wires that receive radio signals from the air

blackmail when a person is forced to give up information or money to prevent personal information from being revealed

bugs small electronic devices used to record sound

CIA the Central Intelligence Agency, the main American spy agency operating outside the United States

classified containing secrets that only certain people are allowed to see

controllers people who organize and run the work of spies

cryptography the science of making and breaking codes

dead drop a public place where spies can drop messages and parcels for each other

double agent a spy pretending to serve one government while actually serving another

fortress a building that is used to protect soldiers or fighting equipment

hostage a person who is held as a prisoner to be exchanged for something from the enemy

intercept to see or overhear a message or transmission meant for another person

KGB the Russian intelligence and security organization

MI5 the agency in charge of counter-intelligence and security in the United Kingdom

MI6 Britian's foreign intelligence service set up in 1909. Its name is an abbreviation of Military Intelligence, section 6.

microphones devices that pick up, record, and amplify sound

mole a spy who works inside the enemy's spy agency

Morse code an alphabet code made up of combinations of long and short sound signals

Revolutionary War fought from 1775 to 1781, this war separated the American colonies (later the United States of America) from Great Britain

saboteurs people who deliberately destroy or damage enemy property

tapping secretly listening in to someone else's conversation, usually with an electronic bug or device

INDEX

agents   9, 13, 16, 25

blackmail   11, 15

cameras   10, 11, 28, 29

CIA   6, 17, 24, 25

codes   7, 18, 19, 20, 21, 23

controllers   22, 23

cryptography   19

dead drop   22, 23

disguises   7, 9, 24, 29

double agents   16

firearms   7

hackers   28

intelligence agencies   16, 17, 18, 19

lock picks   8

MI5   7

MI6   17

microphone   12, 13

moles   16, 17, 29

Morse code   20, 21

phone tapping   13

radios   7, 20, 21

saboteurs   27

satellite   29

undercover 14, 15

WEB FINDER

International Spy Museum
www.spymuseum.org
Hundreds of pages of spy stuff, from secret equipment to spy stories and tales of famous spies

Spy Technology—Dialogue for Kids
www.idahoptv.org/dialogue4kids/season4/spy/
Learn more about the secret language of spies.

CIA
https://www.cia.gov/kids-page/index.html
Look into what it takes to be a spy for the CIA and what they do day to day.